MUSIC OF THE STARS

SONGS RECORDED BY BARBRA STRE

RARE JAZZ AND POPULAR SONGS FROM THE AMERICAN S

VOLUME 9

T0061342

Produced by John L. Haag

Sales and Shipping:

PROFESSIONAL MUSIC INSTITUTE LLC

1336 Cruzero Street, Box 128
Ojai, CA 93024
info@promusicbooks.com

Free Again

(Non... C'est Rien)

English Lyric and Musical Adaptation by Robert Colby
French Lyric by Michael Jourdan
Music by Armand Canfora and Joss Baselli

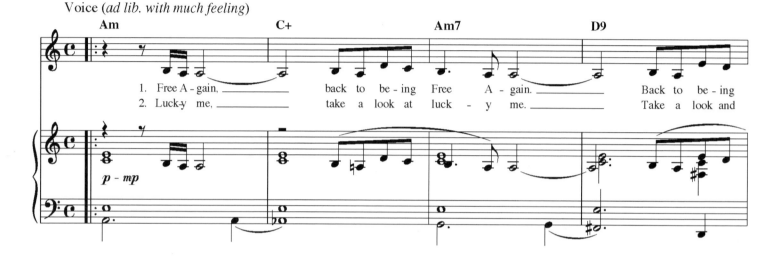

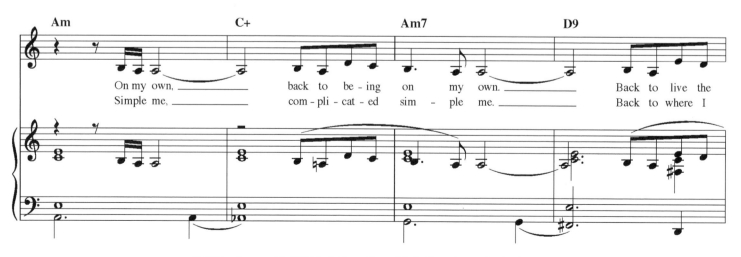

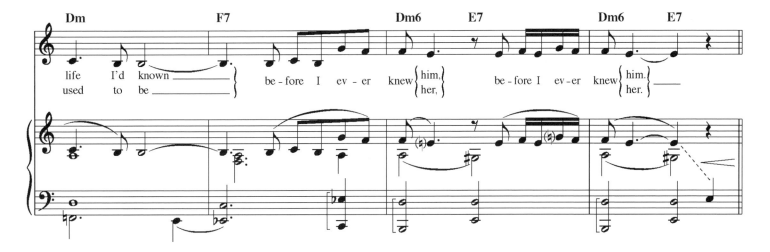

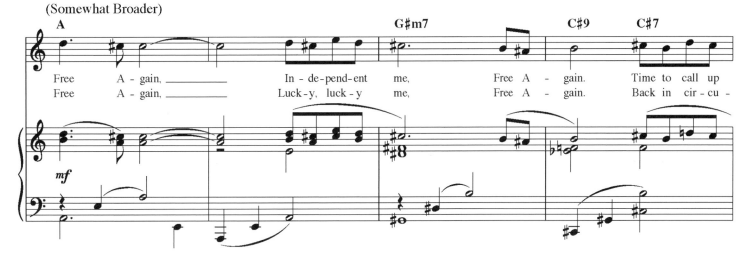

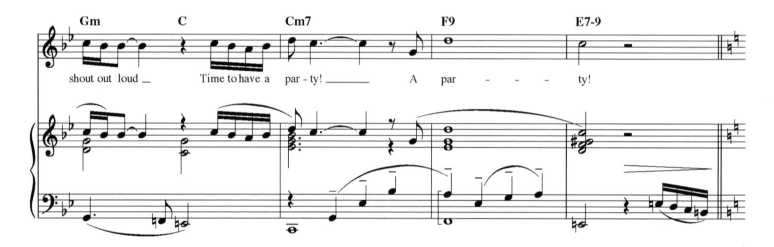

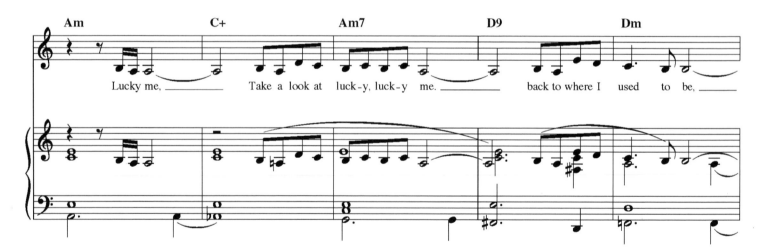

Non... C'est Rien

(Free Again)

English Lyric and Musical Adaptation by Robert Colby
French Lyric by Michael Jourdan
Music by Armand Canfora and Joss Baselli

Non, c'est rien
Ou si peu croyez-le bien,
Ça ira mieux dès demain
Avec le temps qui passe
Dans la vie, tout s'efface
Non, c'est rien
A quoi bon tendre vos mains?
Je n'ai pas tant de chagrin
C'est vous qui êtes tristes
Mes amis, partez vite.

Laissez-moi
Cette nuit sortez
Mais sans moi
Allez boire à ma santé
Remportez vetre pitié
Vous me faites rire
Bien rire.

Non, c'est rien
Ou si peu croyez-le bien
Cet amour n'était plus rien
D'autre qu'une habitude
J'en ai la certitude
Non, c'est rien
Ce garçon moi, je le plains
Ne croyez pas que demain
Une seule seconde
Je serai seule au monde.

Laissez-moi
Cette nuit sortez
Mais sans moi
Allez boire à mes amous
A tous mes futurs amours
Mes prochains "Je t'aime"
"Je t'aime".

Laissez-moi
Et ne croyez pas,
Surtout pas,
Que je vais pleurer pour ça,
Seul mon coeur n'y comprends rien.
Mais à part ça rien,
Rien!

Non, c'est rien
Ou si peu croyez-le bien
Je n'ai pas tant de chagrin
Je n'ai pas tant de chagrin
Non, c'est rien
Non, c'est rien
Rien.

(Have I Stayed)
Too Long At The Fair ?

Lyric and Music by
Billy Barnes

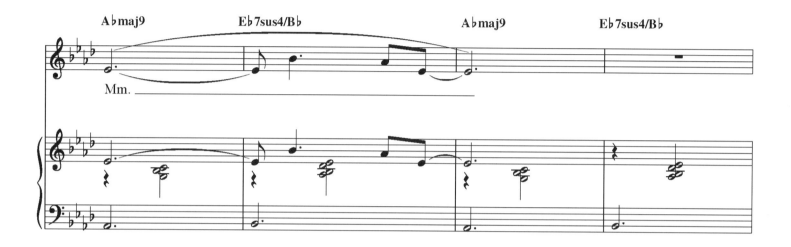

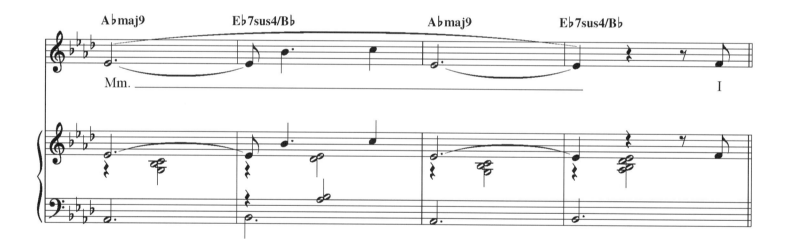

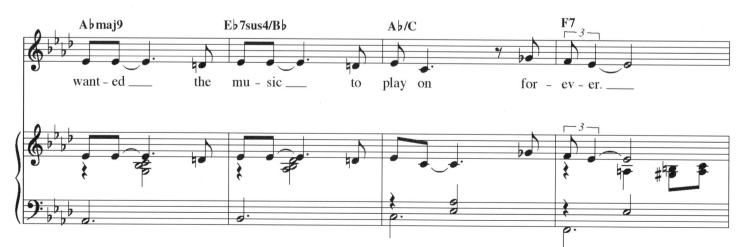

rib - bons _____ to tie up _____ my hair, but I _____

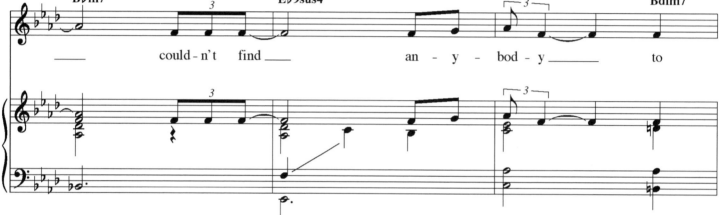

_____ could - n't find _____ an - y - bod - y _____ to

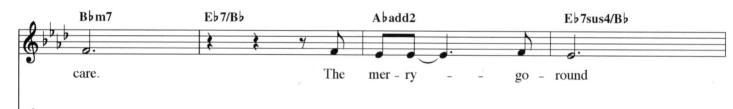

care. The mer - ry - - go - round is be - gin - ning to slow now. _____

is be - gin - ning to slow now. _____ Have I stayed too long _____

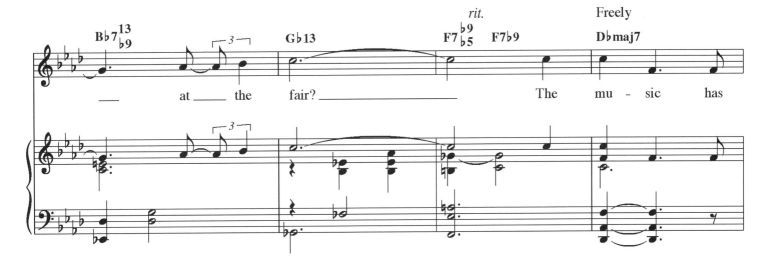

at _____ the fair? _____ The mu - sic has

stopped and the chil - dren _____ must go _____ now. Have

I stayed too long at the fair? _____

Oh, moth-er dear, ____ I know you're ver - y proud. ___ Your

lit - tle girl ___ in ging - ham is ___ so far a - bove the crowd.

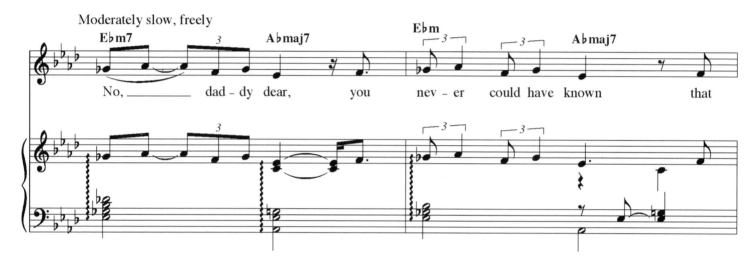

Moderately slow, freely

No, ___ dad - dy dear, you nev - er could have known that

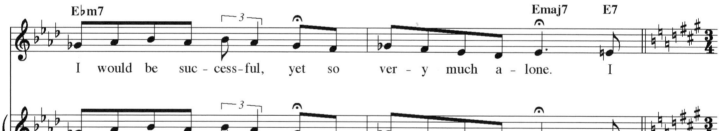

I would be suc - cess - ful, yet so ver - y much a - lone. I

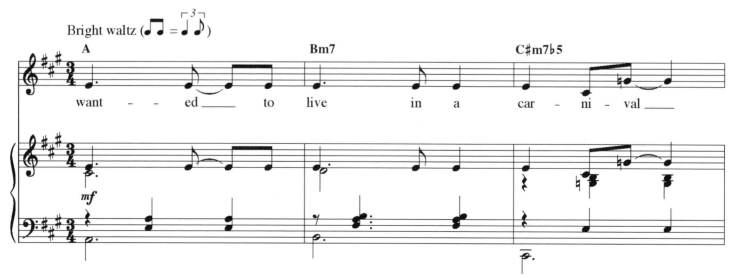

Bright waltz

want - - ed ___ to live in a car - ni - val ___

cit - y _____ with laugh - ter, _____ love _____ ev - 'ry - where. _____

I want - ed my friends _____ to be thrill - ing and

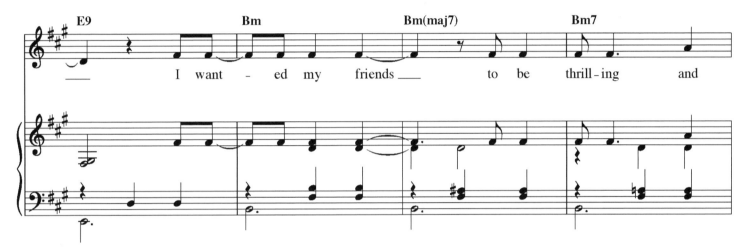

wit - ty. _____ I want - ed some - bod - y to care. _____

Slowly, freely

I found my blue rib - bons _____ all shin - y _____ and

Too long at the fair ? 6-8

There is noth-ing to win. And there's no one to

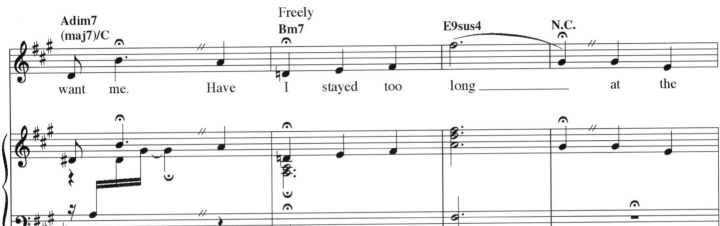

want me. Have I stayed too long at the

fair?

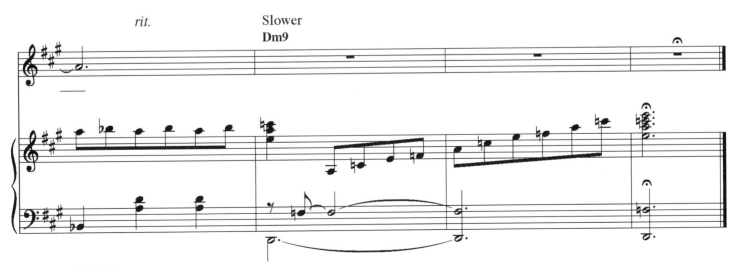

Keepin' Out Of Mischief Now

(From The Broadway Musical "Ain't Misbehavin")

Lyric by Andy Razaf
Music by Thomas "Fats" Waller

Don't e-ven go ___ to a mov-ie show, _
Don't go for an - y ex - cite-ment now ___

If you are not ___ at my side;
Books are my best ___ com-pa - ny

I just stay home ___ by my ra - di - o, _
All my o - pin - ions have changed some - how ___

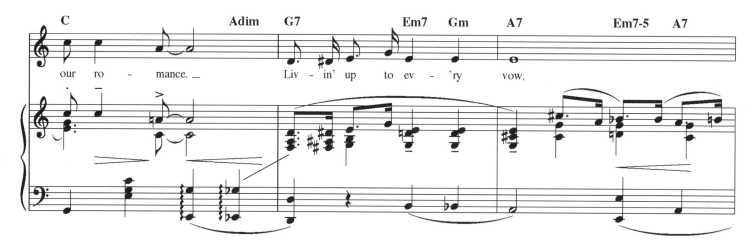

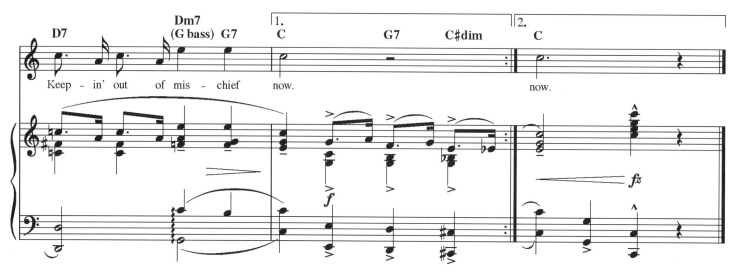

But Beautiful

Lyric by Johnny Burke
Music by Jimmy Van Heusen

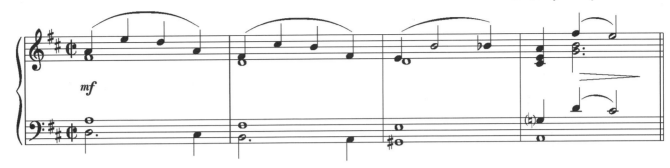

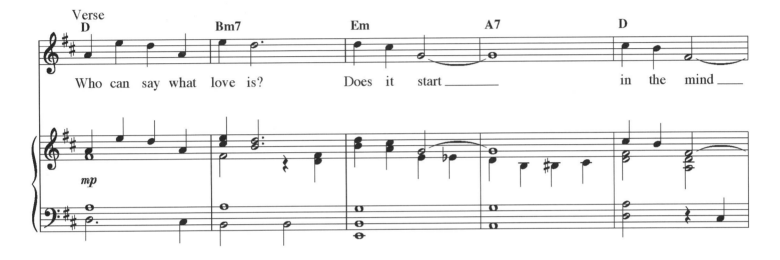

Who can say what love is? Does it start _____ in the mind _____

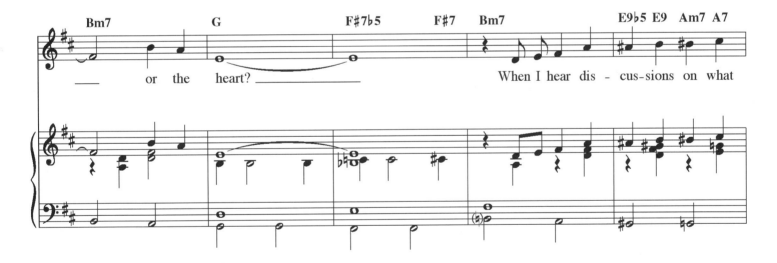

_____ or the heart? _____ When I hear dis - cus-sions on what

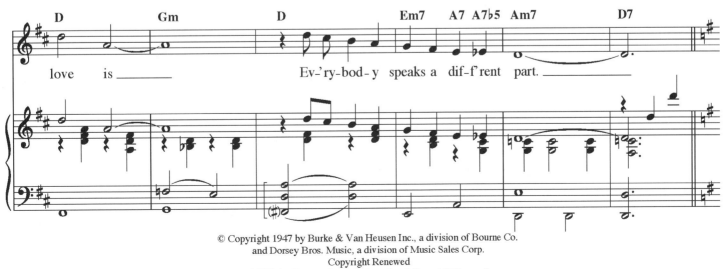

love is _____ Ev-'ry-bod-y speaks a dif-f'rent part. _____

Refrain *(Slowly with expression)*

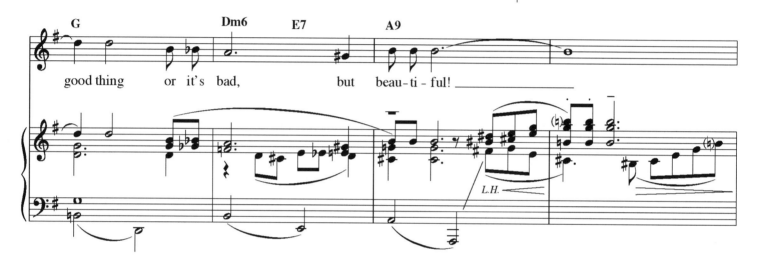

Love is fun-ny or it's sad Or it's qui-et or it's mad; It's a

good thing or it's bad, but beau-ti-ful! _____

Beau-ti-ful to take a chance and if you fall, you fall And I'm

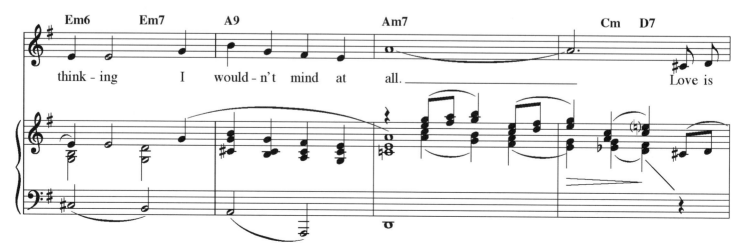

think-ing I would-n't mind at all. _____ Love is

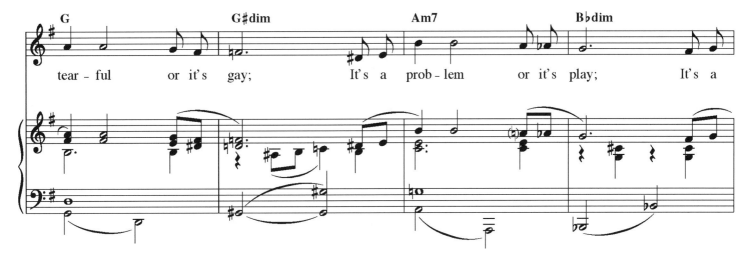

tear - ful or it's gay; It's a prob - lem or it's play; It's a

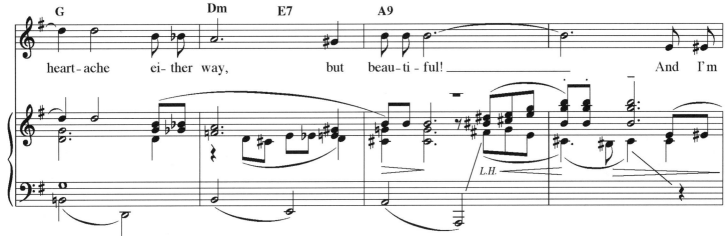

heart - ache ei - ther way, but beau - ti - ful! _____ And I'm

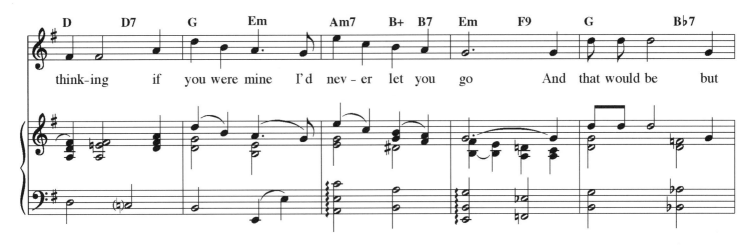

think - ing if you were mine I'd nev - er let you go And that would be but

beau - ti - ful I know. _____ Love is know. _____

But beautiful 3-3

For All We Know

Lyric by Haven Gillespie
Music by J. Fred Coots

Moderately slow

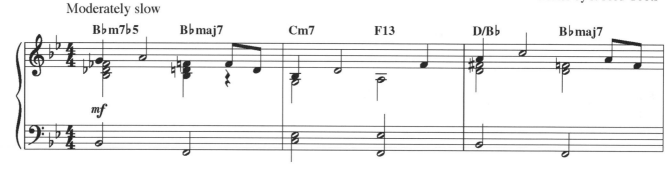

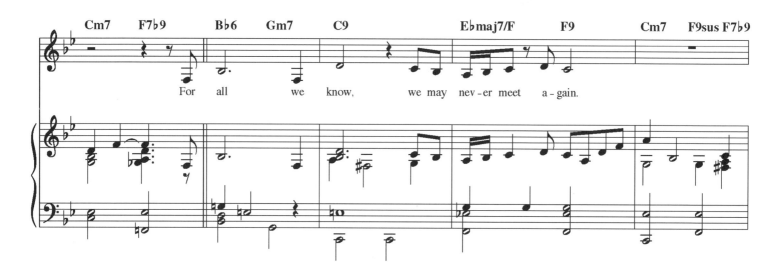

For all we know, we may nev-er meet a-gain.

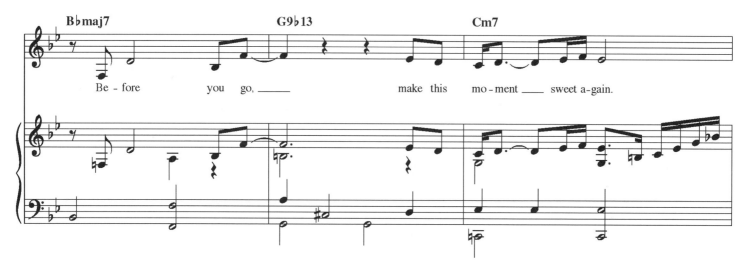

Be-fore you go, _____ make this mo-ment _____ sweet a-gain.

We won't _____ say good-bye

un - til ___ the last ___ min-ute.   I ___ might hold ___ out my ___ hand

and check   'cause my heart's gon-na be in it.   Oh, _____ for

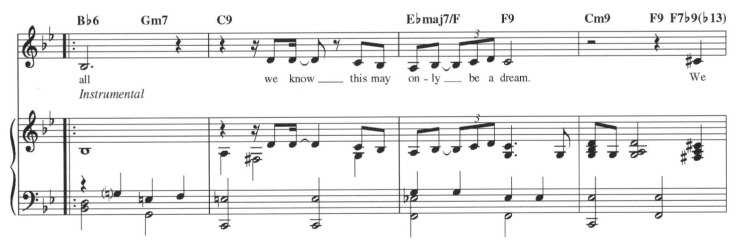

all   we know ____ this may on - ly ___ be a dream.   We

Instrumental

come   and we go   like a rip-ple   on a stream.

Instrumental Ends   So,

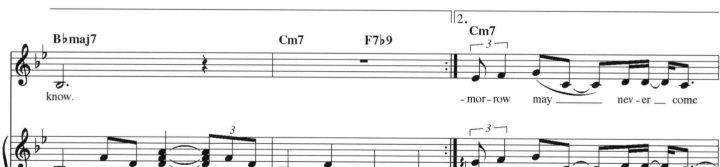

It Had To Be You

(from the Motion Picture "When Harry Met Sally")

Lyric by Gus Kahn
Music by Isham Jones

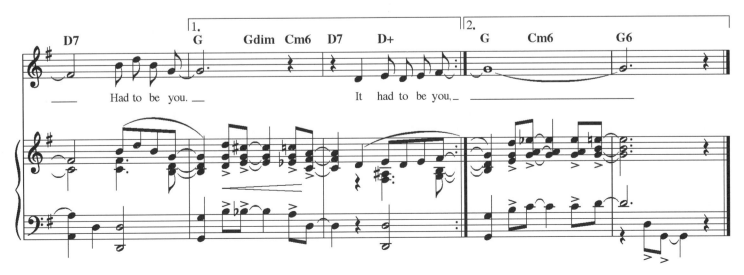

It had to be you 3-3

The Best Things In Life Are Free

Lyric and Music by
B. G. DeSylva, Lew Brown and Ray Henderson

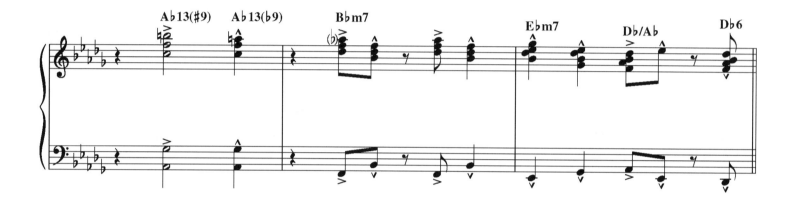

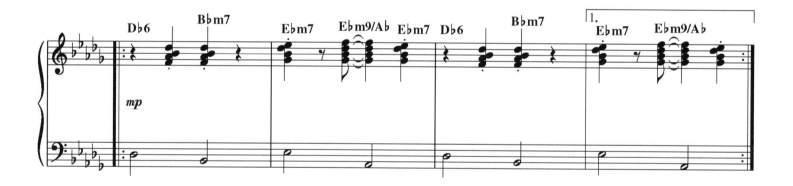

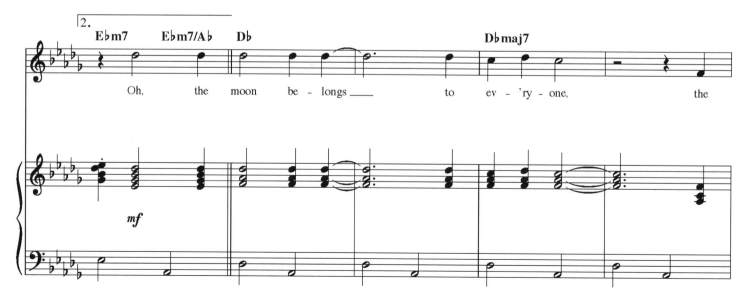

Oh, the moon be - longs ___ to ev - 'ry - one, the

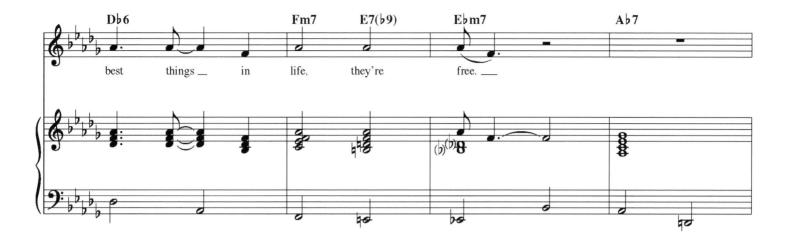

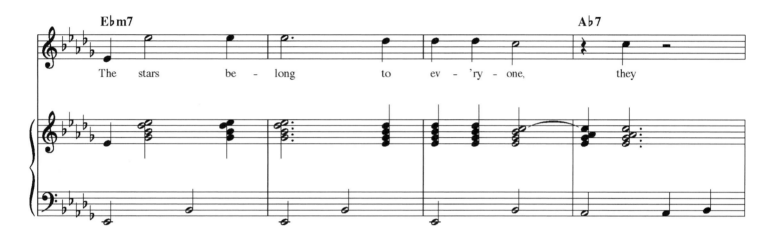

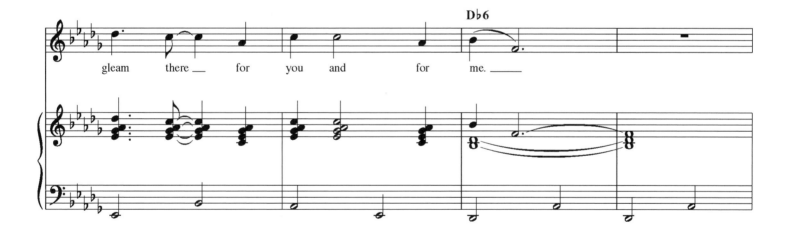

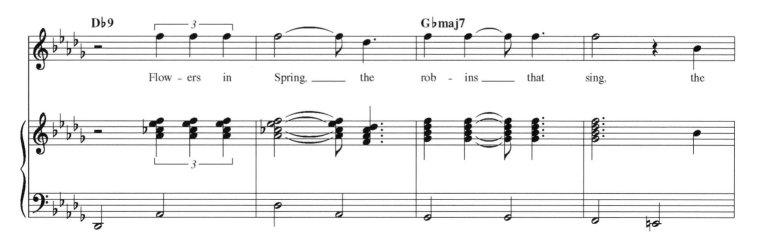

The best things in life are free 2-6

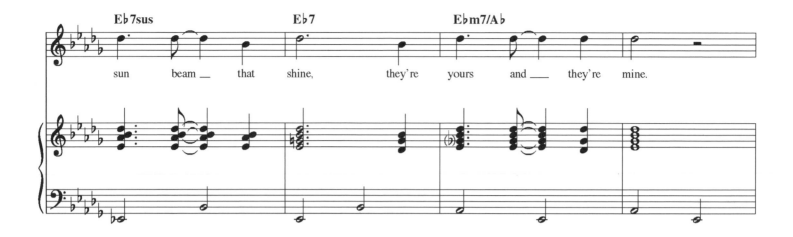

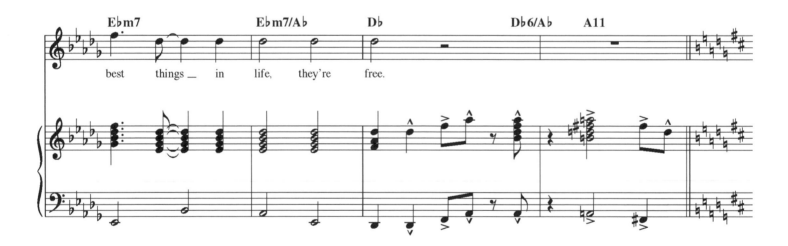

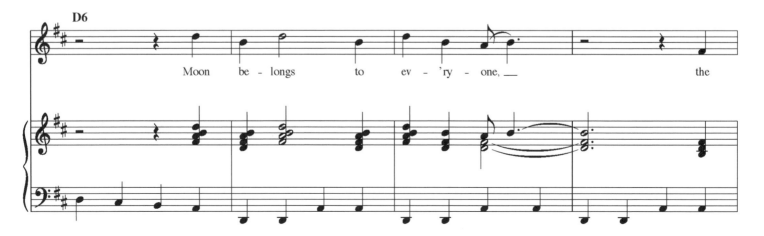

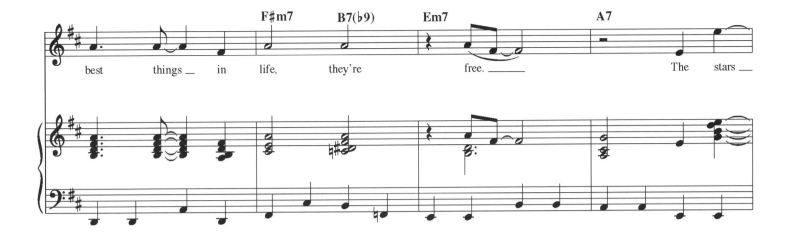

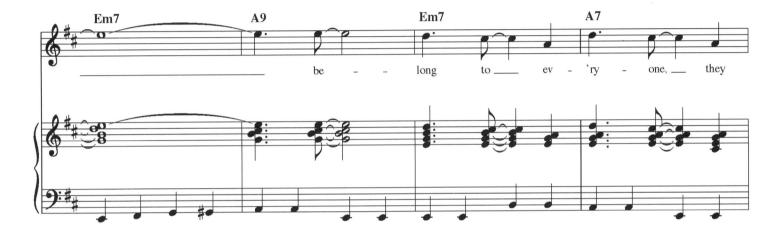

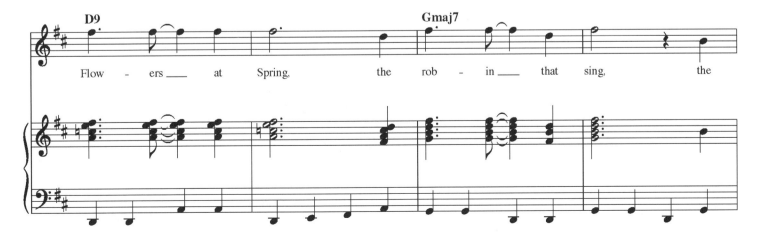

The best things in life are free 4-6

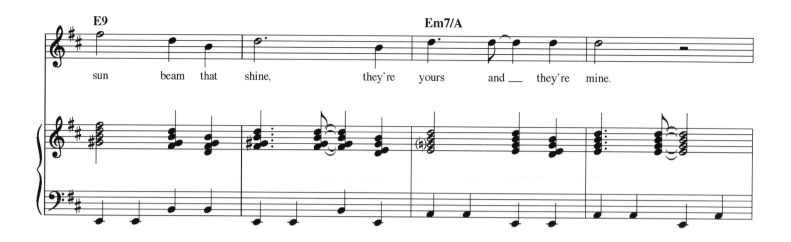

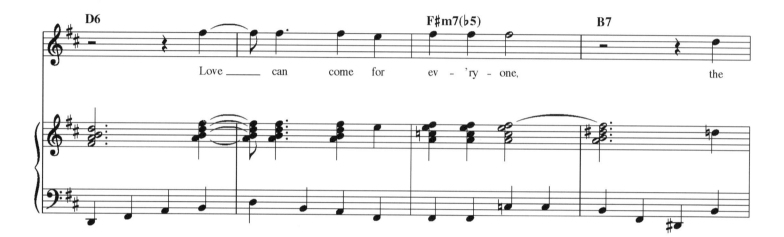

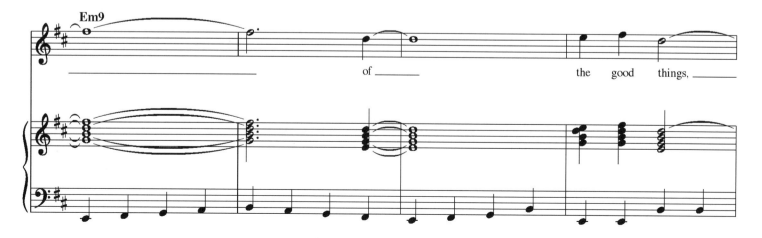

The best things in life are free 5-6

ev - 'ry - one ___ of ___ the bet - ter things, ___ the

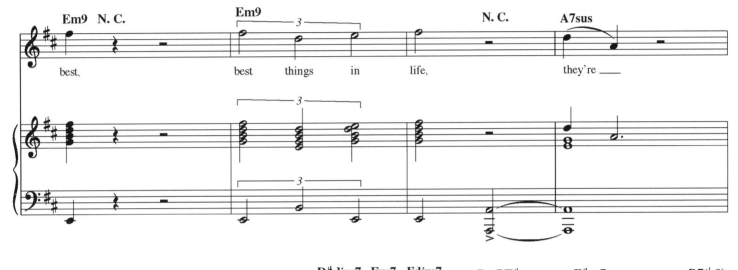

best, best things in life, they're ___

free. ___

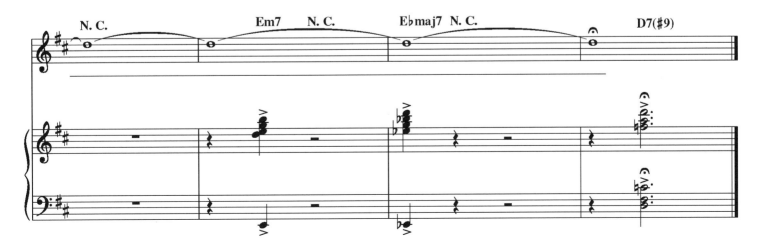

My Man

English Lyric by Channing Pollock
French Lyric by Albert Willemetz and Jacques Charles
Music by Maurice Yvain

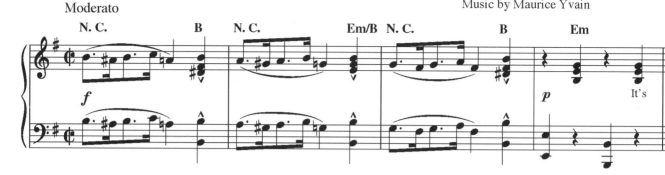

cost me a lot, but there's one thing that I've got, _____ it's my man.
Somt - times I say if I just could get a - way with _____ my man
Sur cet - te terr' ma seul joie, mon seul bon-heur C'est mon hom - me,

Cold and wet, tired you bet; but all that I soon for - get with _____
He'd go straight sure as fate, for it nev - er is too late for _____
J'ai don - né tout c'que j'ai, mon a - mour et tout mon coeur, A mon

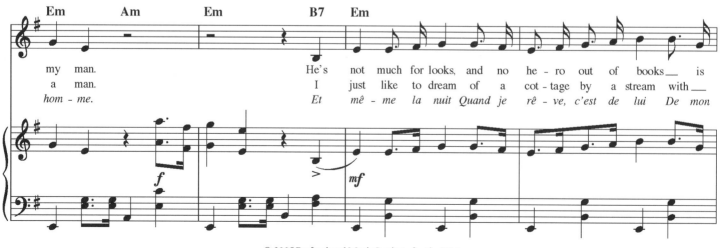

my man.   He's not much for looks, and no he - ro out of books__ is
a man.   I just like to dream of a cot - tage by a stream with __
hom - me.   Et mê - me la nuit Quand je rê - ve, c'est de lui De mon

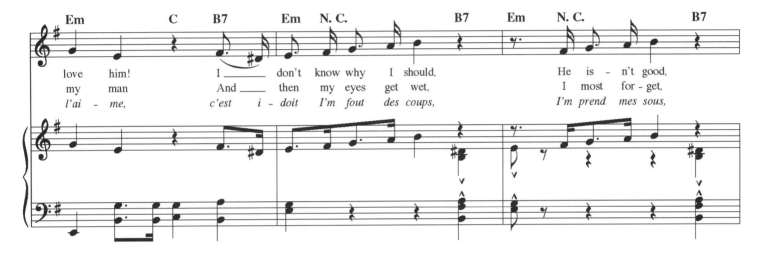

My man 2-3

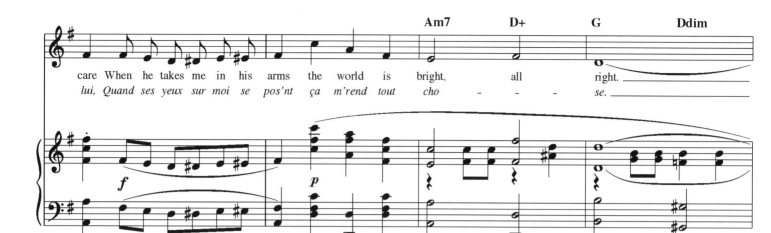

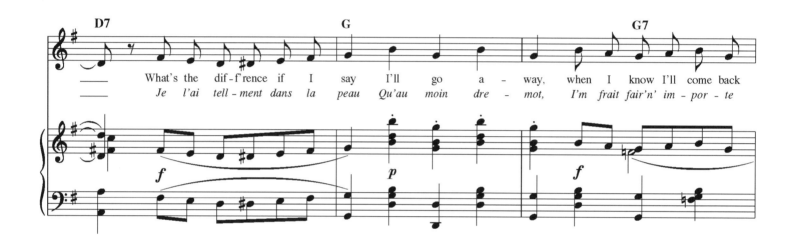

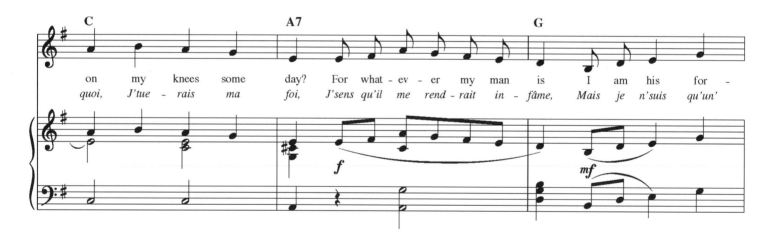

More Than You Know

Lyric by Billy Rose and Edward Eliscu
Music by Vincent Youmans

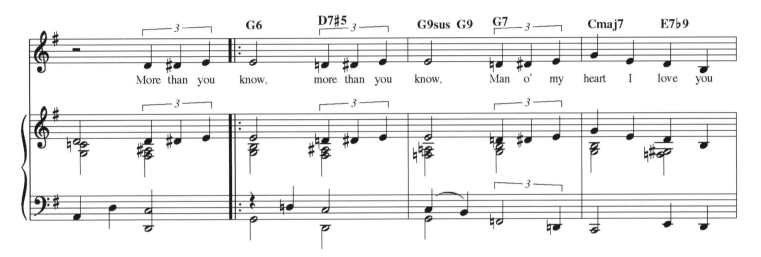

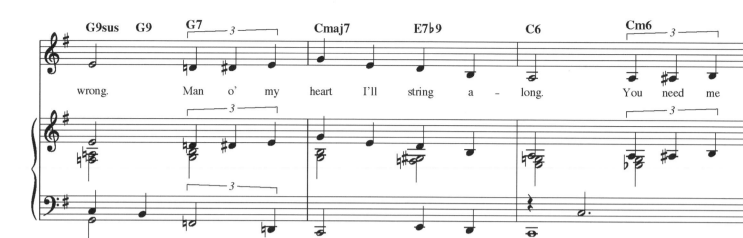

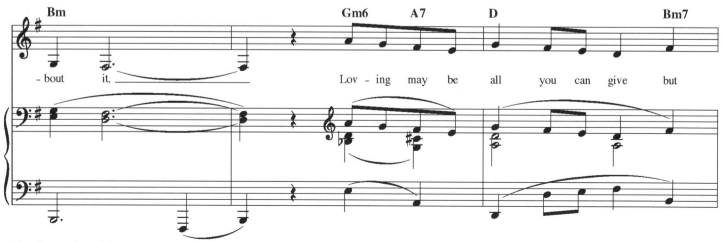

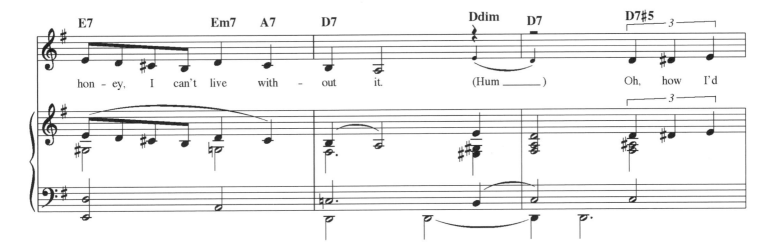

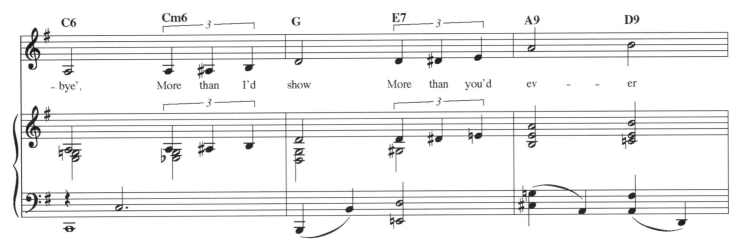

My Buddy

Lyric by Gus Kahn
Music by Walter Donaldson

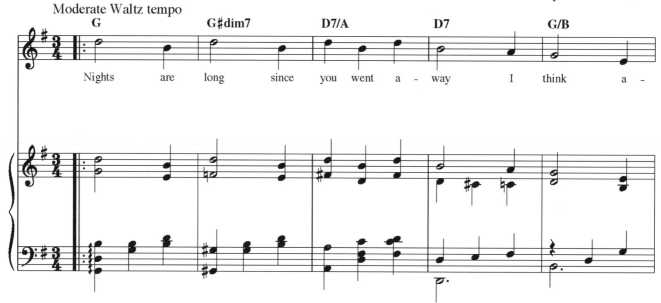

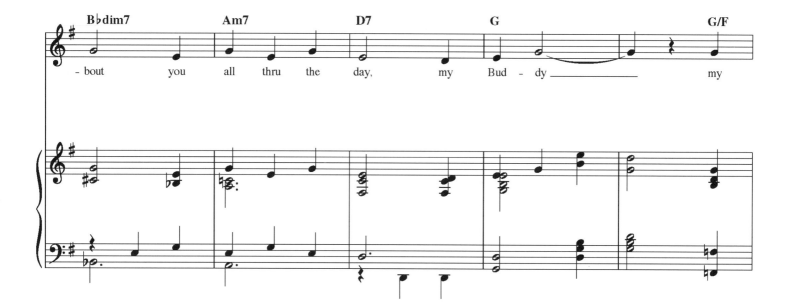

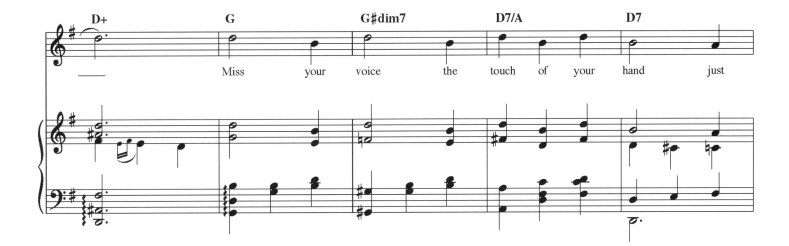

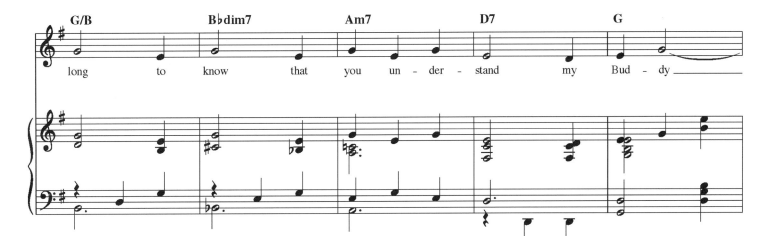

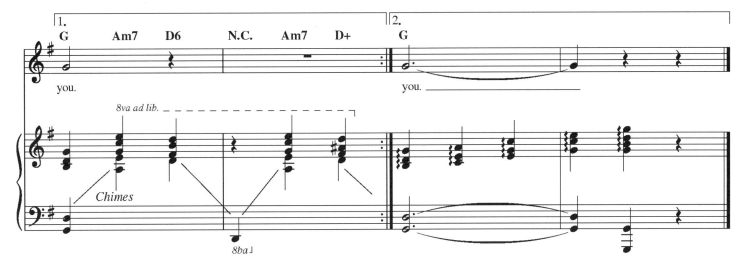

My Buddy 2-2

I've Got No Strings

(from Walt Disney's "Pinocchio")

Words by Ned Washington
Music by Leigh Harline

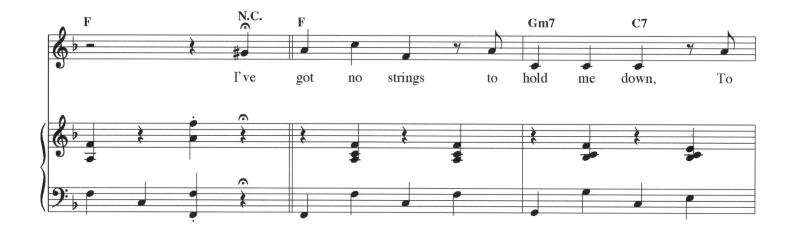

I've got no strings to hold me down, To

make me fret, or make me frown, I had strings But

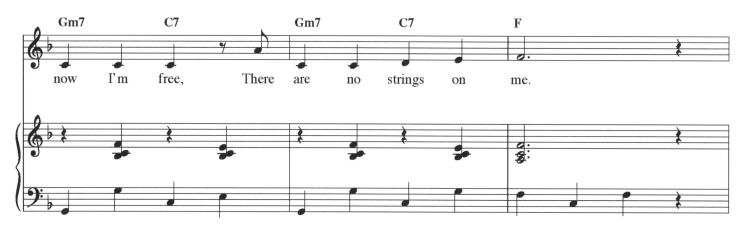

now I'm free, There are no strings on me.

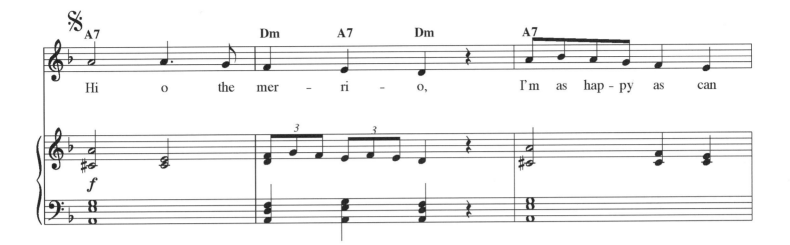

Hi o the mer – ri – o, I'm as hap - py as can

be. I want the world to know

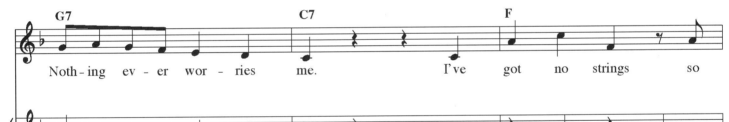

Noth - ing ev - er wor - ries me. I've got no strings so

I have fun, I'm not tied up to an – y – one,

To Coda

How I love my lib-er-ty, There are no strings on me.

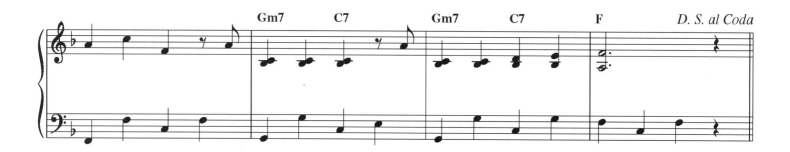

(Instrumental interlude)

D. S. al Coda

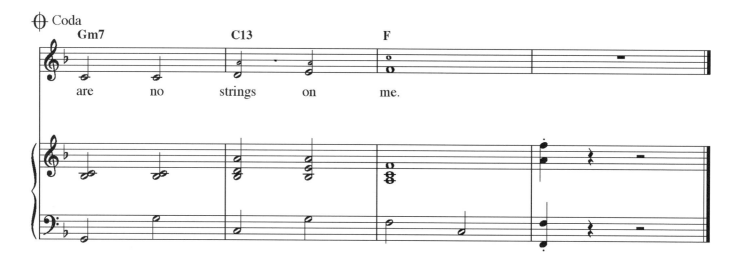

Coda

are no strings on me.

Second Hand Rose

Lyric by Grant Clarke
Music by James F. Hanley

44

Second hand rose 2-5

Refrain - Moderato, not too slowly

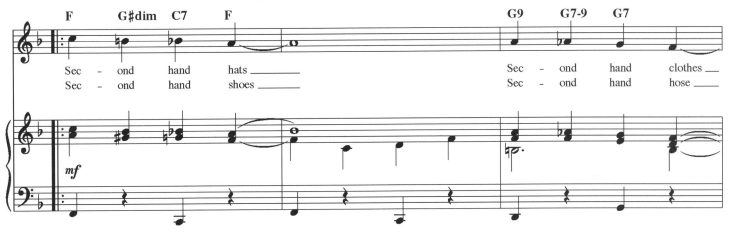

Sec - ond hand hats _____ Sec - ond hand clothes _____
Sec - ond hand shoes _____ Sec - ond hand hose _____

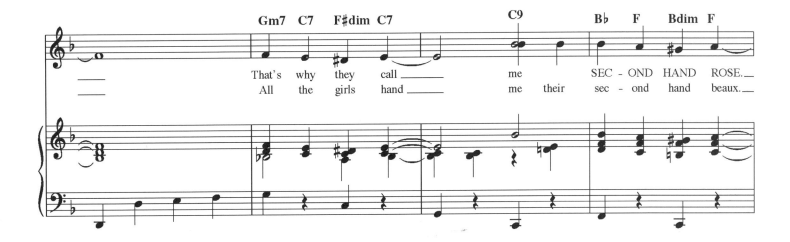

That's why they call _____ me SEC - OND HAND ROSE. _____
All the girls hand _____ me their sec - ond hand beaux. _____

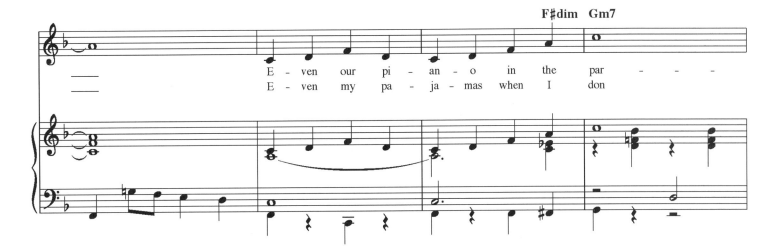

E - ven our pi - an - o in the par - - -
E - ven my pa - ja - mas when I don

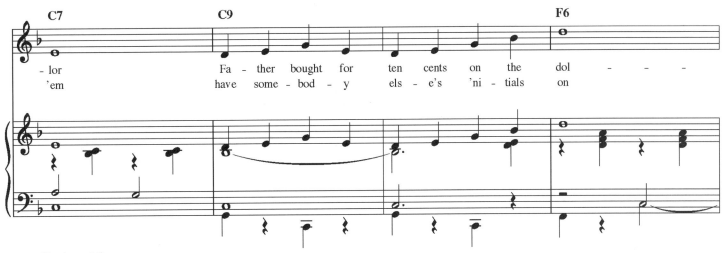

- lor Fa - ther bought for ten cents on the dol - - -
'em have some - bod - y els - e's 'ni - tials on

Second hand rose 3-5

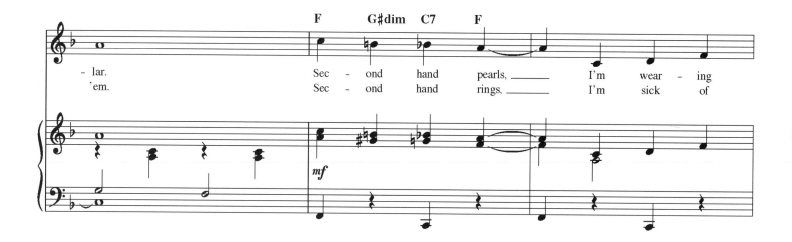

Second hand rose 4-5

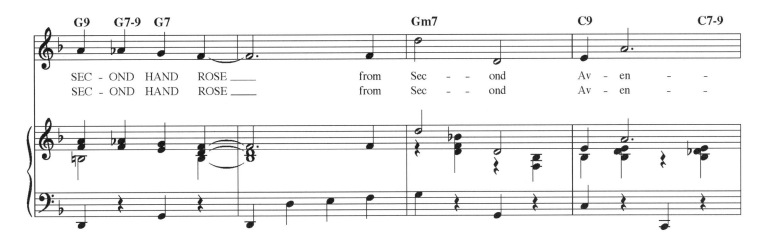

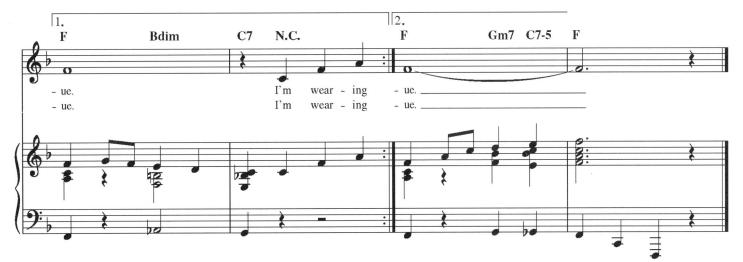

Second hand rose 5-5

(There's Gonna Be A)
Great Day
(From the Musical "Great Day!")

Lyric by Billy Rose and Edward Eliscu
Music by Vincent Youmans

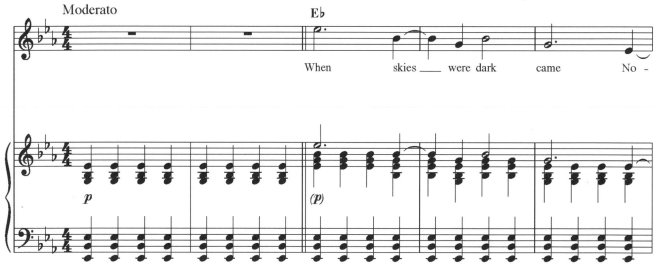

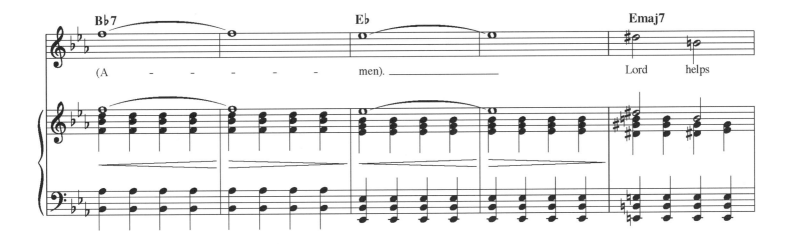

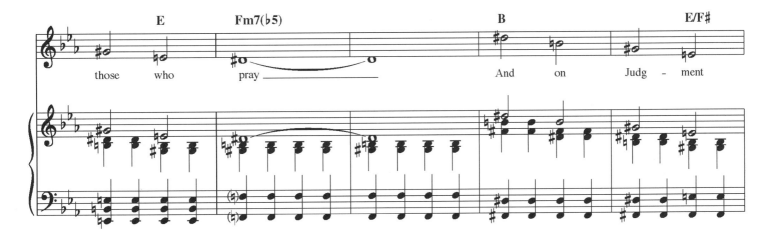

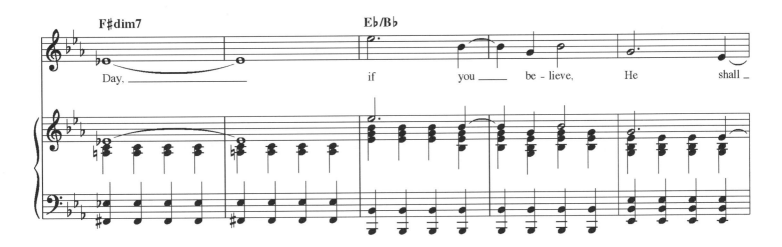

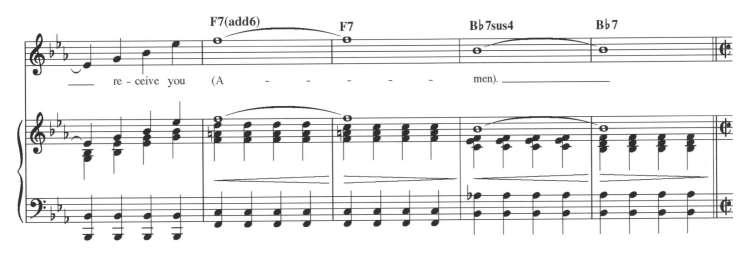

Great day 2-4

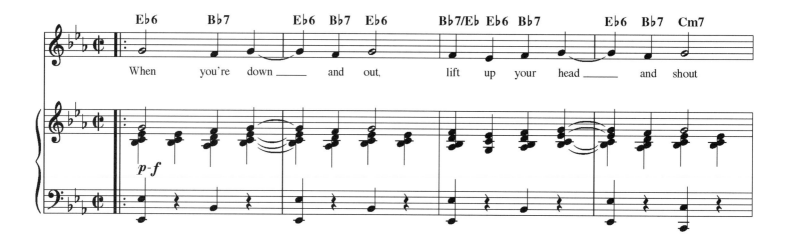

When you're down ____ and out, lift up your head ____ and shout

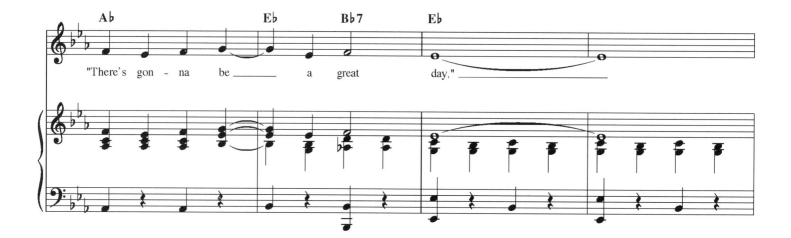

"There's gon - na be ____ a great day," ____

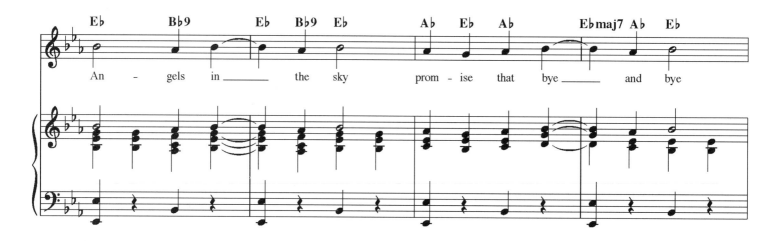

An - gels in ____ the sky prom - ise that bye ____ and bye

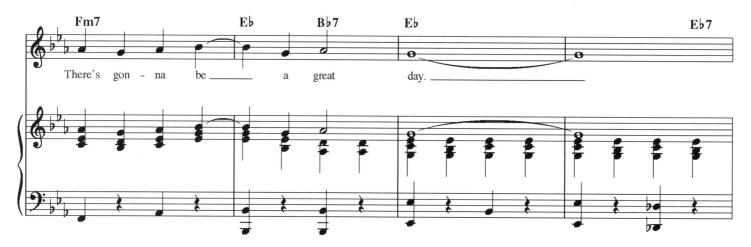

There's gon - na be ____ a great day. ____

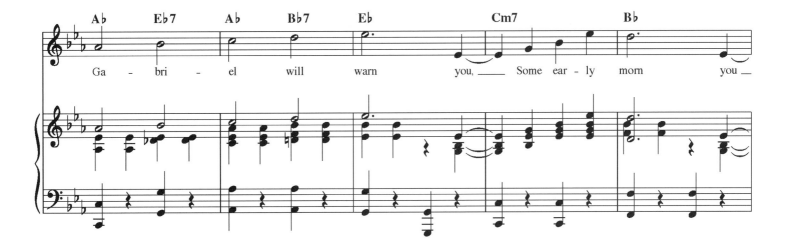

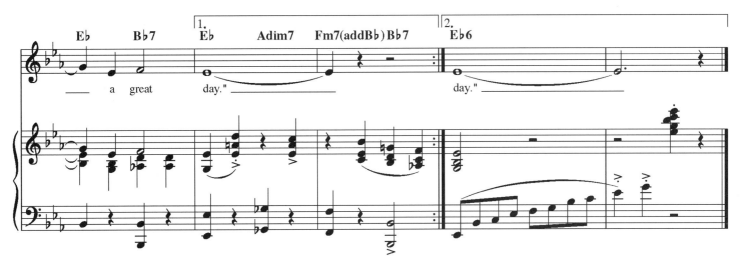

Great day 4-4

They Didn't Believe Me

Lyric by Herbert Reynolds
Music by Jerome Kern

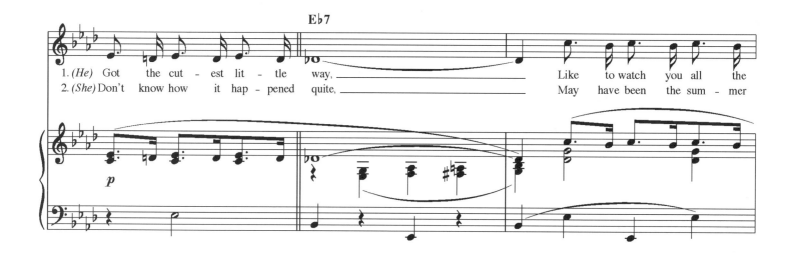

1. (He) Got the cut-est lit-tle way, _____ Like to watch you all the
2. (She) Don't know how it hap-pened quite, _____ May have been the sum-mer

day _____ And it cer-tain-ly seems fine _____ Just to think that you'll be
night _____ May have been, well, who can say _____ Things just hap-pen an-y

mine. _____ When I see your pret-ty smile _____
way, _____ All I know is I said "yes!" _____

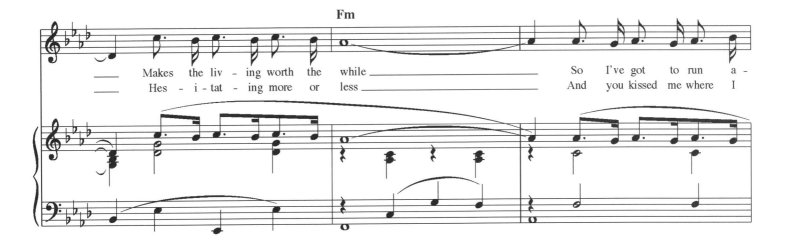

Makes the liv - ing worth the while ___ So I've got to run a -
Hes - i - tat - ing more or less ___ And you kissed me where I

- round ___ Tell - ing peo - ple what I've found. ___
stood ___ Just like an - y fel - low would. ___

Refrain

(He) And when I told them ___ How beau - ti - ful you are ___
(She) And when I told them ___ How won - der - ful you are ___

___ They did - n't be - lieve me ___ They did - n't be - lieve me! ___
___ They did - n't be - lieve me ___ They did - n't be - lieve me! ___

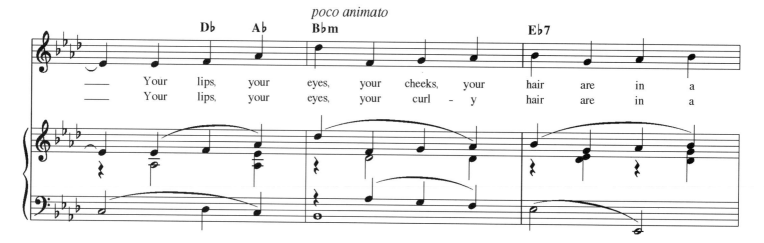

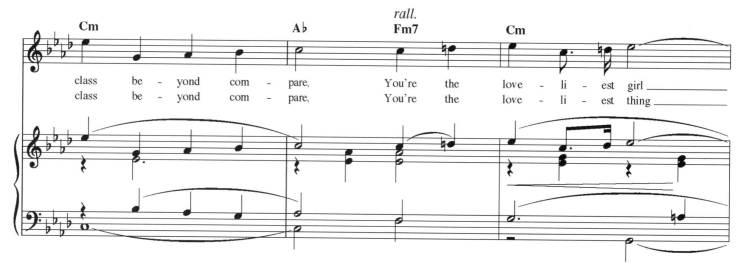

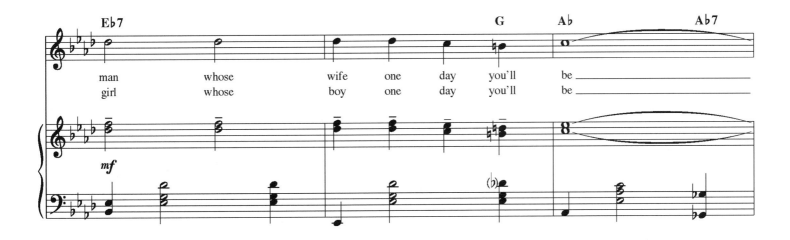

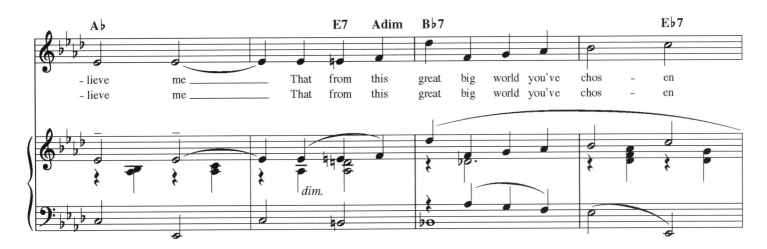

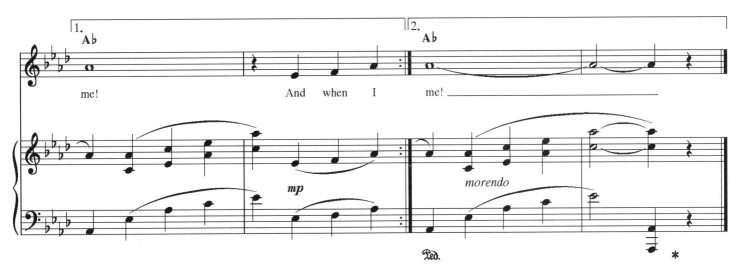

man whose wife one day you'll be _____
girl whose boy one day you'll be _____

_____ They'll nev - er be - lieve me, _____ They'll nev - er be -
_____ They'll nev - er be - lieve me, _____ They'll nev - er be -

- lieve me _____ That from this great big world you've chos - en
- lieve me _____ That from this great big world you've chos - en

1. me! And when I
2. me! _____

They didn't believe me 4-4

Taking A Chance On Love

Lyric by Ted Fetter and John LaTouche
Music by Vernon Duke

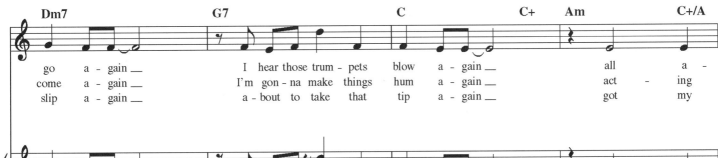

Taking a chance on love 2-4

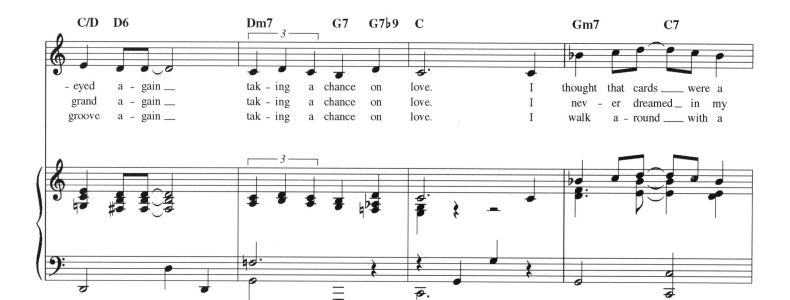

Taking a chance on love 3-4

My Honey's Loving Arms

Lyric by Herman Ruby
Music by Joseph Meyer

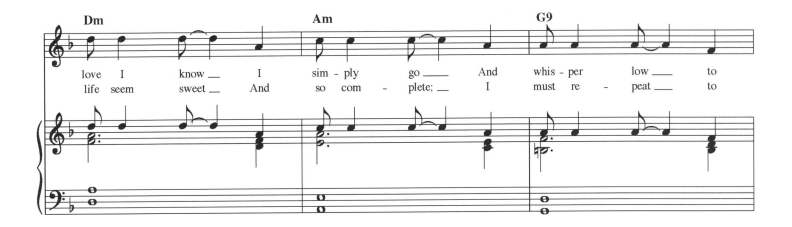

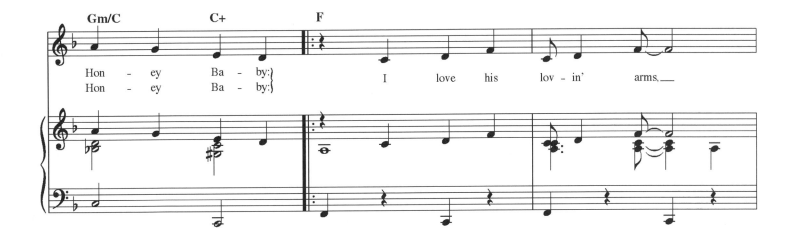

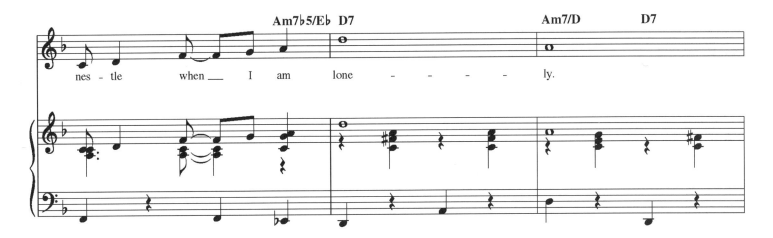

My honey's loving arms 2-4

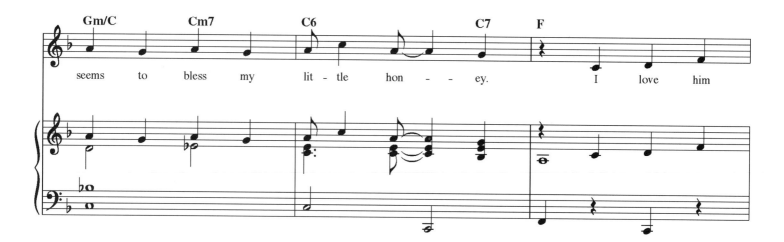

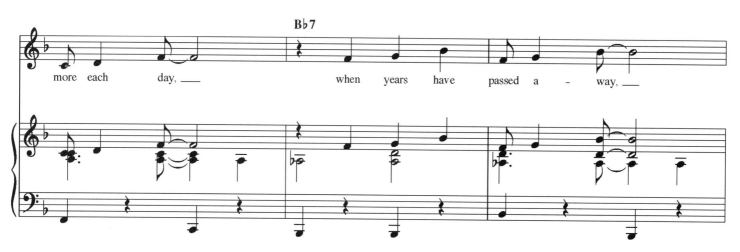

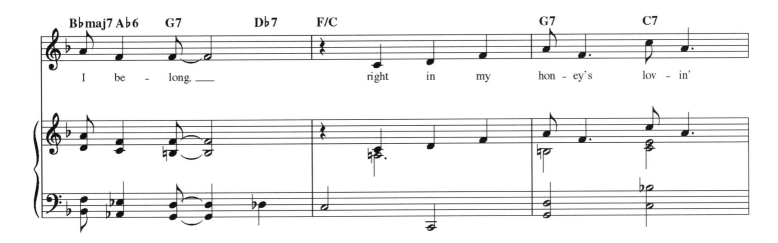

My honey's loving arms 4-4

Some Day My Prince Will Come

(from Walt Disney's "Snow White and the Seven Dwarfs")

Words by Larry Morey
Music by Frank Churchill

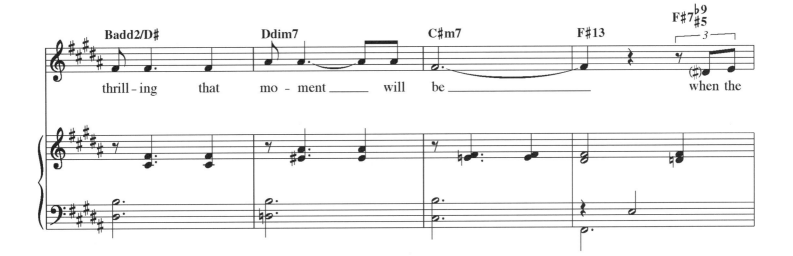

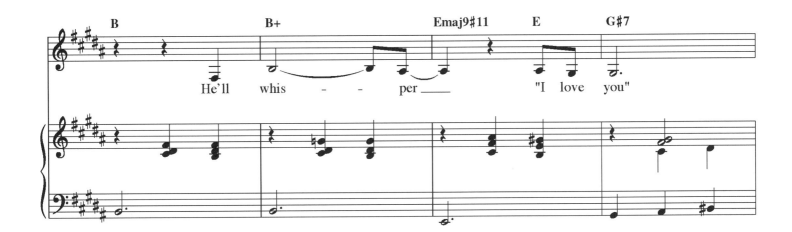

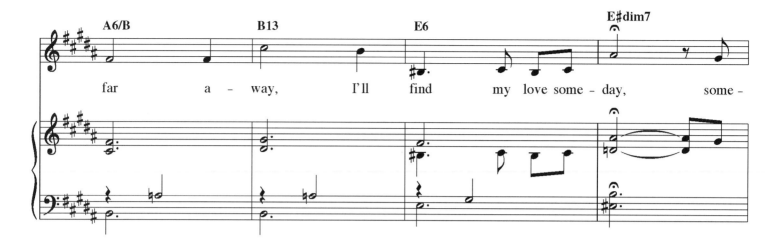

far a - way, I'll find my love some - day, some -

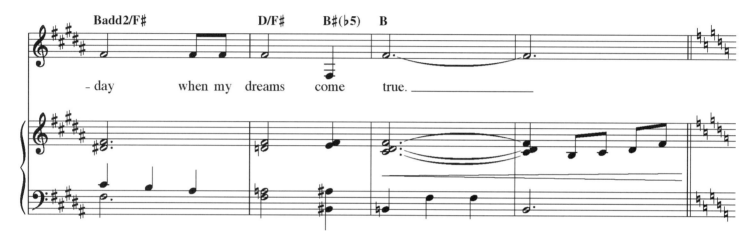

- day when my dreams come true. _____

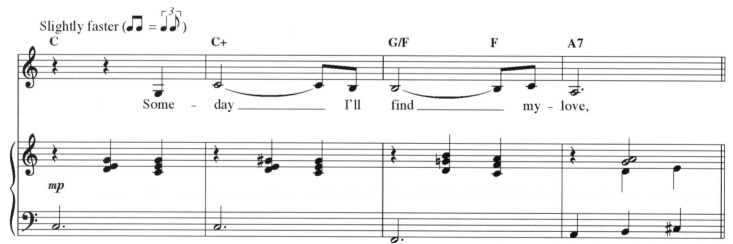

Slightly faster

Some - day _____ I'll find _____ my - love,

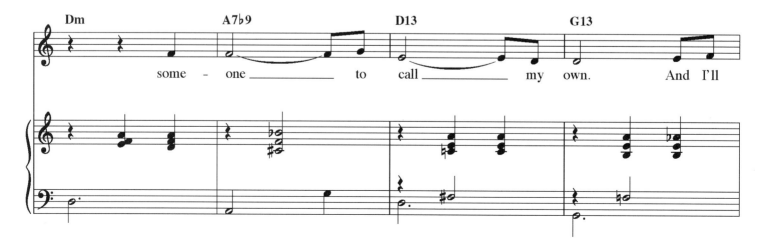

some - one _____ to call _____ my own. And I'll

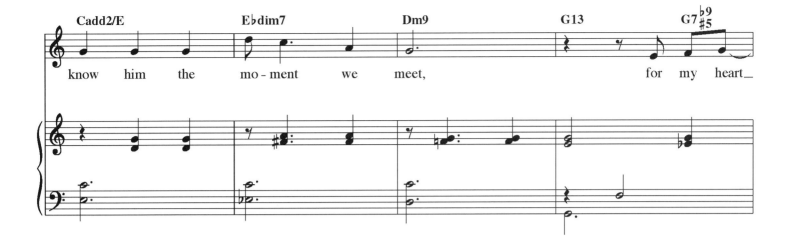

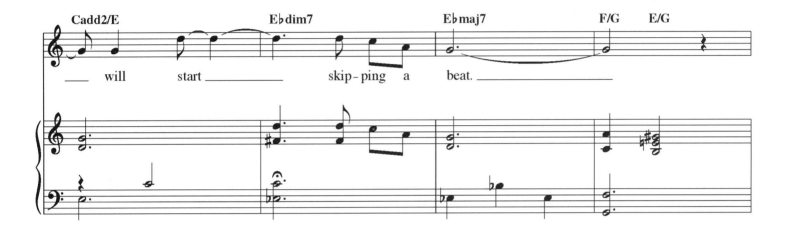

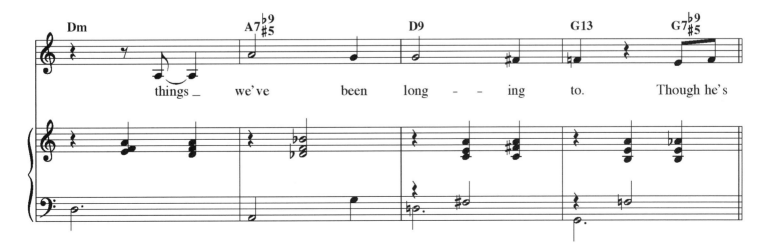

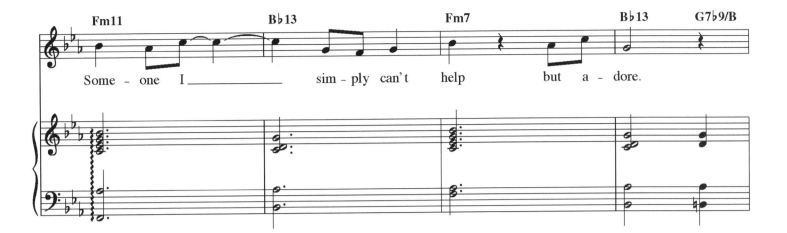

Some - one I _____ sim - ply can't help but a - dore.

Some - one who'll thrill me for - ev - - - er. _____

_____ Some - day _____ my prince will come.

Some - - day I will find the one. Though he's

What Now My Love

(French Title: "Et Maintenant"))

English Lyric by Carl Sigman
French Lyric by Perre Leroyer
Music by Gilbert Becaud

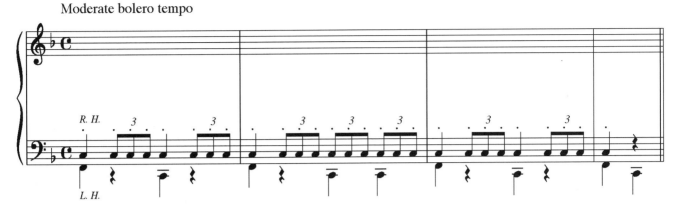

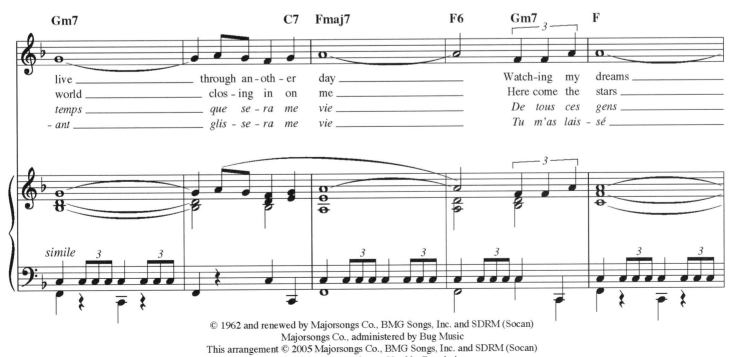

What now my love 2-3

Who's Afraid Of The Big Bad Wolf?

(from Walt Disney's "The Three Little Pigs")

By Frank E. Churchill
Additional Lyric by Ann Ronell

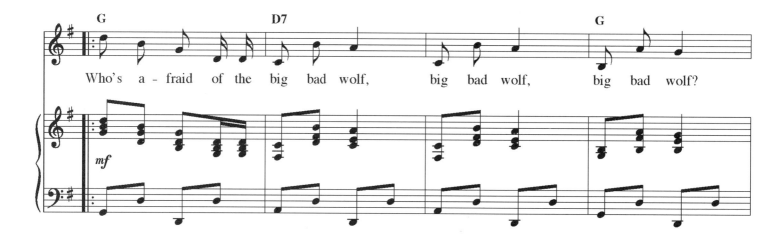

Who's a-fraid of the big bad wolf, big bad wolf, big bad wolf?

Whos' a-fraid of the big bad wolf? Tra la la la la. la. Long a- / Came the

-go, there were three pigs, Lit-tle handsome pig-gy-wigs, For the big bad, very big,
day when fate did frown, And the wolf blew in-to town, With a gruff "puff, puff," he

played on his fiddle and danced with la - dy pigs; Num - ber three said, "Nix on
fast un - locked and said, "Come in with me!" Now they all were safe in -

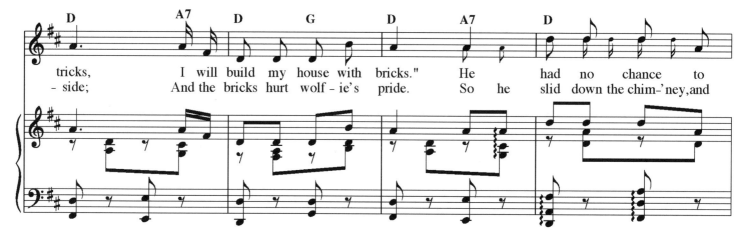

tricks, I will build my house with bricks." He had no chance to
- side; And the bricks hurt wolf - ie's pride. So he slid down the chim - 'ney, and

sing and _ dance, 'Cause _ work and play don't mix! Ha - Ha Ha! The
oh, by Jim-'ney, In the fi - re he was fried! Ha - Ha Ha! The

two little, do little pigs Just winked and laughed Ha - Ha!
three little, free little pigs Re - joiced and laughed Ha - Ha!

Who's a-fraid of the big bad wolf, big bad wolf, big bad wolf?

Who's a-fraid of the big bad wolf, Tra la la la la.

Who's a-fraid of the big bad wolf, big bad wolf, big bad wolf?

Who's a-fraid of the big bad wolf? Tra la la la la. Long
Came the

la.

Smile

(From the Motion Picture "Modern Times")

Lyric by John Turner and Geoffrey Parsons
Music by Charles Chaplin

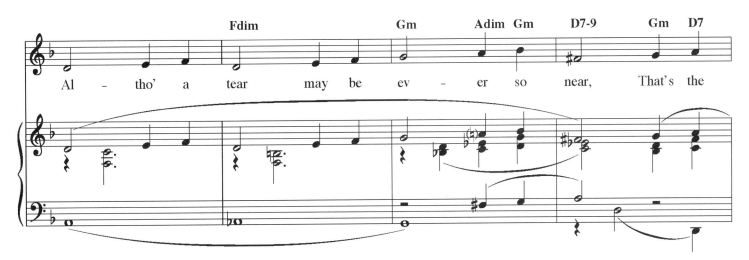